I0019123

THE BASICS OF DATA
GOVERNANCE

Epris E. Ezekiel

Table of Contents

Introduction

The planning, supervision, and management of data, as well as the utilization of data and data-related resources, as well as the creation and execution of policies and decision-making authority over data use, constitute data governance. An enterprise data management or enterprise information management program's foundation is this.

Information technology (IT) governance differs from data governance. IT governance makes decisions about IT investments, applications, and projects. Data governance exclusively emphasizes the management of information and data assets. Data governance and IT governance practices (such as information security and privacy) may need to included in some enterprise issues.

Data governance includes people, corporate processes, and procedures that guarantee organizations can improve data quality, deliver data value, develop and maintain data and its metadata, and make the right data available to the right people in the right format at the right time. As a result, data governance can be thought of as creating guidelines and standards for gathering, recognizing, keeping, and utilizing the resource known as "data." A robust, ongoing data governance program takes time to develop and maintain.

All data governance schemes essentially have the same objectives:

- ✓ Assure openness in the data governance and management processes.
- ✓ Lower the expenses and boost the efficiency of data utilization and management

- ✓ Establish guidelines and procedures that enable cooperative and common data management.
- ✓ Teach employees and management to embrace and apply standard data management techniques.
- ✓ At all organizational levels, lessen the operational friction brought on by a lack of data and process governance.
- ✓ Facilitate safe and efficient decision-making regarding data and information resource management.

Chapter 1

What is Data Governance?

Data governance is the framework of decision-making authority and accountability for information-related procedures, carried out by established models that specify who has the authority to do what, with what information, when, under what conditions, and with what techniques. Enterprise enterprises must prioritize data governance because of the intricacy and dispersion of data assets. Guaranteeing the quality, security, and accessibility of data helps businesses stay competitive and make well-informed decisions.

Proper data governance is crucial for enterprises to manage their data assets effectively and efficiently. It offers a strong foundation for data management, guaranteeing that information is correct, comprehensive, and uniform throughout the company. Organizations may ensure that their data is safe and complies with applicable laws and standards by putting in place robust data governance procedures. In addition to reducing hazards, this improves the data's general credibility, which is essential for operational effectiveness and strategic decision-making.

The significance of data governance

The resolution of data inconsistencies across many systems within an organization may be impossible without efficient data governance. Sales, logistics, and customer service systems, for instance, occasionally list customer names differently. Failure to solve that could lead to operational challenges in those departments, impede data integration efforts, and generate data integrity problems that impact the quality of corporate reporting, data science applications, and business intelligence (BI). Additionally, data inaccuracies may go unnoticed and uncorrected, which would further impair the accuracy of analytics.

Poor data governance might also hamper initiatives to comply with regulations. That might be problematic for businesses that adhere to the growing number of data privacy and protection regulations, such as the California Consumer Privacy Act (CCPA) and the GDPR of the European Union. The creation of standard data formats and common data standards that are used in all business systems is usually part of an enterprise data governance effort. This improves data consistency for business purposes and helps comply with regulatory requirements.

Why Organization need Govern Data

1. To prevent disparities in data among departments and business units

2. For a consistent understanding of data, it is necessary to agree on standard data definitions.

3. To enhance the quality of data by attempting to find and correct problems in data sets

4. To provide dependable information to decision-makers and improve analytical correctness

5. Enforcing and putting into practice procedures that assist stop data abuse and inaccuracies

6. To assist in guaranteeing adherence to regulations and data privacy laws

Who is in charge of data governance?

The data governance process involves various individuals in most businesses. These comprise end users who are knowledgeable about the pertinent data domains in an organization's systems, as well as business executives, data management specialists, and IT personnel. These are the main players and their main roles in governance.

Data guardians.

One of the duties of data stewards is supervising and maintaining data sets. They are also responsible for making sure that end users follow the rules and policies that have been authorized by the data governance committee. The data stewardship function is typically assigned to employees who are knowledgeable about specific data assets and domains. In some organizations, that is a full-time role; in others, it is a part-time one. A combination of business data stewards and IT stewards may also exist.

Chapter 2

Committee or council for data governance.

However, the governance team often does not decide on standards or policies. The data governance council or committee, which is mainly composed of company executives and other data owners, is in charge of that. The core data governance policy, related policies and regulations on topics like data access and usage, and the processes for putting them into practice are all approved by the committee. It also settles conflicts, including those involving data definitions and formats that arise between several business divisions.

Manager and team of data governance. In certain situations, the CDO or a comparable executive—for instance, the director of enterprise data management—may also serve as the program manager for the practical aspects of data governance. In others, companies designate a special data governance manager or lead to oversee the initiative. The program manager usually leads a full-time data governance team that works on the initiative. Coordinating the process, conducting meetings and training sessions, monitoring metrics, handling internal communications, and performing other management duties are all part of what is often more formally referred to as the data governance office.

Chief information officer.

A data governance program's chief data officer (CDO), if one exists, is frequently the senior executive in charge of it and bears significant accountability for its success or failure. In addition to gaining the program's approval, money, and staffing, the CDO is responsible for spearheading its establishment, overseeing its advancement, and serving as an internal advocate. In the absence of a CDO, a C-suite executive will typically act as an executive sponsor and perform the same duties.

Typically, the governance process also includes data architects, data modelers, data quality analysts, and engineers. To help them avoid utilizing data incorrectly or improperly, analytics teams and business users also need to be trained on data governance policies and data standards.

Benefits of Data Governance

1. Clear, useful, and doable procedures for efficiently using, maintaining, and feeding data are necessary to provide appropriate training and ongoing knowledge transfer about data management.

2. Use certified data to increase the value of current data across teams.

3. Organization-wide, centrally sourced guidelines, and standards for transactional and enterprise definitions of data and their changes.

4. To create and preserve a uniform corporate language, the entire business should have access to an enterprise glossary and a data dictionary (metadata management).

5. Procedures that are laid out and carried out for gathering data, defining problems, and resolving conflicts related to data.

6. By defining and recording the needs of every business sector that uses information, an appropriate enterprise strategy for data management may be adopted.

7. knowledge, communication, and comprehension of corporate goals, particularly those about information and data use, such as managing and classifying an organization's data assets to make search and discovery easier.

8. knowledge management that is thorough and consistent across the company through the management of data and metadata (definitions, context, etc.).

Chapter 3

Frameworks for Data Governance

A systematic method for managing data assets, a data governance framework offers a collection of guidelines, rules, and practices. Typical data governance frameworks consist of the following essential elements:

- ❖ **Metrics and Monitoring for Data Governance:** These offer a means of gauging and tracking the efficacy of data governance, encompassing data security, compliance, and quality. Organizations can track their success and pinpoint areas for development with the use of metrics and monitoring tools.

- ❖ **Roles and Duties of Data Governance:** These outline the duties and obligations

14

of the people and groups participating in data governance, such as data owners, data users, and data stewards. Clearly defined roles facilitate accountability and guarantee efficient management of data governance responsibilities.

❖ **Procedures for Data Governance:** These describe the procedures and stages involved in data management, such as data input, processing, storage, and disposal. Procedures give data handling a clear road map and guarantee that all tasks are carried out in a consistent and regulated way.

❖ **Data Governance Guidelines:** These outline the policies and procedures for managing data, including security, accessibility, and quality. Policies guarantee that information is handled in an organization-wide, responsible manner.

Selecting the appropriate framework for your company

The size and complexity of your company, the kind and volume of data you handle, and your unique data governance requirements all play a role in selecting the best data governance framework. Several well-liked frameworks for data governance include:

❖ **Data Governance Institute (DGI) Framework:** An organized method for managing and governing data that was created especially for data governance. The DGI Framework provides comprehensive instructions for setting up and sustaining efficient data governance procedures.

❖ **COBIT (Control Objectives for Information and Related Technology):** A popular framework for managing and governing IT, which includes data governance. A thorough method for overseeing and managing business IT environments is offered by COBIT.

❖ **ISO 27001 (Information Security Management System):** A framework for managing information security that covers data governance and security. Establishing, implementing, maintaining, and continuously improving an information security management system is made easier for enterprises by ISO 27001.

Take into account the following elements while selecting a data governance framework:

❖ **Industry Acceptance & Recognition:** Select frameworks that are commonly accepted and used in your sector; these are probably more stable and dependable.

❖ **Requirements for Cost and Resources:** Analyze the human and financial resources required for the framework's adoption and maintenance.

❖ **Implementation and Maintenance Simplicity:** Take into account the resources needed for both implementation and continuing upkeep. Long-term sustainability will be higher for a framework that is simple to establish and maintain.

❖ **Conformity to the aims and objectives of your organization:** Make sure the framework can be incorporated into your current procedures and supports your strategic goals.

❖ **Flexibility and Scalability:** Select a framework that can grow with your company and adapt to your evolving data governance requirements.

Effective data management and governance can be supported by a strong data foundation that you can create by carefully choosing a data governance framework that fits the requirements of your company.

In data governance, master data management

For an organization to have a consistent, accurate version of the truth, master data management, or MDM, is necessary. MDM guarantees data consistency across departments and systems by centralizing data assets, connecting different sources, and eliminating redundant data entries. Important results include:

* **Security and Regulatory Compliance:** A strong MDM system improves overall quality and data security standards by enabling businesses to adhere to regulatory requirements for sensitive data through access restrictions and security measures.

* **Enhanced Cooperation:** Whether in data-driven business intelligence projects or initiatives for a personalized customer experience, MDM promotes efficient collaboration between data teams and various departments, providing correct and comprehensive data for better results.

* **Encouragement of Digital Transformation:** By enabling machine

learning, data visualization, and analytics projects, an efficient MDM approach smoothly interacts with digital technologies, putting businesses in a position to innovate and adapt swiftly.

- ❖ **Improved Organizational Understanding:** Business stakeholders can transparently access the organization's data assets through a consolidated master data repository. Strategic business objectives are supported and well-informed decision-making is made possible by this degree of data integrity.

- ❖ **Consistency and Accuracy of Data**: MDM procedures ensure reliable data throughout the organization's systems by defining uniform standards for data entry and data lineage.

Implementing master data management inside a data-driven culture affects how a business organizes, shares, and utilizes its data. This foundation provides scalable analytics, generates decreased costs through efficient data management, and enables better decision-making across departments.

Chapter 4

Benefits of a Data Foundation

A solid data foundation enables businesses to scale and adjust to changing data requirements, as well as more successfully utilize emerging technologies. Setting up architecture and infrastructure that promotes scalability, performance, and security requires optimized data storage. Teams may collaborate easily across departments using reliable, accurate data thanks to this foundation's streamlined procedures and increased operational efficiency. Important advantages include:

- ❖ **Constant Improvement:** To sustain continued relevance and efficacy, a well-maintained data foundation incorporates new data governance techniques and technologies as it develops over time.

- ❖ **Better Insights and Reporting:** A strong foundation enables businesses to produce accurate reports fast, assisting decision-makers in depending on current data.

- ❖ **Active Problem Identification:** Organizations may reduce risks and facilitate proactive decision-making by quickly identifying and resolving data inconsistencies through effective data integration and lifecycle management.

❖ **The ability to scale and adapt:** Growing data quantities and complexity are supported by a strong data foundation. As the company expands or incorporates additional data sources, it becomes crucial.

❖ **Increased Efficiency in Operations:** A strong data foundation streamlines processes, enhancing accuracy and speeding up data processing, which lowers operating expenses and unnecessary work.

Data Stewardship vs. Data Governance

Data governance offers the organizational definition, procedures, and guiding principles

24

needed to protect and improve the data asset. Professionals in data management and data governance carry out this task.

With the help of data management and data governance experts, as well as industry standards and best practices for data management, data stewardship empowers the organization to make wise, consistent decisions based on business people's understanding of the data they use daily.

The person in charge of carrying out the guidelines and standards created by the data governance organization is known as a data steward. A data steward is typically an employee of a company who has extensive knowledge of a certain topic or functional area (such as accounting, product, or customer data). By the guidelines and standards established by the data governance program, business data stewards strive to enhance the quality of data (content) and metadata (context) for the organization's vital data. Data stewardship and data governance are complementary, not interchangeable.

Important Success Elements for Effective Data Stewardship and Governance

Any organization's success in implementing data governance and data stewardship is not guaranteed. The long-term viability of any data governance program and the data stewardship role depends on the following elements:

. It is necessary to set up efficient training programs to instruct not only the data stewards but also everyone they interact with.

✓ The organization creates and maintains data policies and standards and regularly follows them.

- ✓ To perform their duties, data stewards and their governing bodies are given an adequate level of authority.
- ✓ The company provides enough resources (people, time, tools, and other technology) to carry out the data stewardship tasks effectively.
- ✓ The position of data stewards within the organizational structure needs to be reviewed regularly and as the number of stewards accepted and involved in planning increases,
- ✓ Periodically planning for the expansion of the Data Governance program staff is necessary, as is adding more data governance professional specialists to support the program's expansion and sustainability.
- ✓ Establishing and maintaining a structured data governance program office with

enough qualified personnel in data management and data governance

✓ Organizational and information technology planning must be closely related to data planning.

✓ Strong and ongoing knowledge of systems management, focus, participation, and assistance in coordinating enterprise information management and data governance with the other areas of information systems and technology management

. Effective and consistent executive management comprehension, focus, participation, and backing for an enterprise data management and data governance program, including enforcing adherence to data-centric policies and data management techniques

Setting Up the Data Governance Role

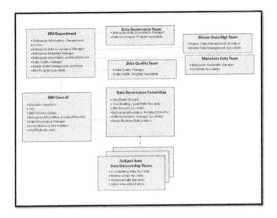

A Basic Organizational Structure Example for Data Governance

Every data governance program requires an organizational structure that complements the enterprise's structure, matches the business's culture, and adheres to industry standards and tried-and-true data governance procedures. It might seem impossible to accomplish all of that. Still, it isn't since there are standard organizational structures for data governance that have been proven to work well in businesses of diverse sizes, sectors, and maturity levels.

Chapter 5

Teams for Data Governance and EIM

The foundation of any successful enterprise data/information management program is the establishment of an Enterprise Information Management Department to oversee the EIM program's operations. This team serves as the central hub for managing and coordinating all enterprise information management operations. All of the information management experts and thought leaders agree that the establishment of such a unit to oversee certain components and manage EIM operations is crucial to the success of enterprise information management (EIM).

As part of the EIM Department, organizations should also establish a dedicated Data Governance unit. The data governance team would begin by creating key roles specifically for enterprise data governance, such as a full-time Data Governance Manager and at least two (2) experienced full-time Data Governance Specialists. As the enterprise program expands to include more than half of the organization's subject areas, more Data Governance Specialists will be required to support it.

Business Data Stewards

It is crucial to remember that not all data in an organization is subject to data governance or data quality management; only data deemed crucial to the decision-making process or the organization's operations are. Twenty to thirty percent of the total data kept in most organizations is mission-critical data. The company must, however, use consistent techniques for managing the governed data to apply metrics and criteria for assessing the program's effectiveness.

For a certain business area (or a subset of an area), the business data stewards are subject matter experts in the data. They enable the data governance specialists to create the rules and guidelines for managing important data by giving them information about the data, including its definition, business meaning, usage trends, etc.

✓ The majority of data stewards are not full-time employees; they have been trained specifically to be corporate data stewards and are identified as such while working in their regular roles (e.g., senior compliance officer, lead underwriter, senior claims analyst, lead financial services representative, etc.).

✓ When it comes to cross-organizational data, a data steward helps find solutions.

✓ Within their area of responsibility, a data steward organizes the advancement of sound data governance procedures.

✓ A data steward possesses or has responsibility for a certain area of the organization and is aware of who handles what data in that area; in other words, they possess local knowledge from a business standpoint (not technical).

Data Governance Standards and Policies

Establishing and upholding the rules and guidelines that apply to all of the enterprise's data falls within the purview of the Data Governance function in the majority of enterprises. Through the use of these policies and standards, the business can specify the quality of its data and conduct operations and decision-making with confidence that its data and information are correct, comprehensive, legitimate, consistent, etc.

The general business rules and procedures that an organization uses to give guidance for the management of data and information are known as data policies. These policies may include documents outlining enterprise data management functions, instructions on how the organization should manage its data, or statements offering guidance for the protection of privileged or confidential data.

For instance:
- ✓ Policies for data and information security (compliance, legal requirements, internal business requirements, etc.)
- ✓ Data Governance Guidelines
- ✓ Policies for Sharing Data (internal and external sources)

✓ Policy for Data Classification

Data standards are the exact requirements, guidelines, and rules that govern how data is specified, created, stored, and used inside an organization. Character length, value ranges, classification categories, and naming conventions are examples of fundamental context pieces for data objects that are included in data standards. For use in a given domain, Data Stewardship teams may provide unique quality metrics, retention guidelines, and backup schedules independently from business data standards.

For instance:

✓ Standards for Data Models
✓ Meta Data Standards (based on ISO 11179)

✓ Based on the characteristics of data quality (accuracy, completeness, validity, consistency, relevance, timeliness, etc.), data quality standards

✓ . Industry, national, and international data standards (such as ISO and HL7)

. Name and address are examples of data format standards.

In order to adhere to a consistent format and facilitate the inclusion of pertinent information (while avoiding superfluous details), policies and standards should be drafted using templates. This will ensure that all stakeholders can comprehend and apply the policies and standards consistently.

Chapter 6

Challenges with data governance

Because different departments within a company frequently have different perspectives on important data entities, such as customers or goods, the initial stages of data governance initiatives can frequently be the most challenging. As part of the data governance process, these discrepancies must be addressed, for instance, by reaching a consensus on standard data definitions and formats. Since that can be a delicate and contentious task, the data governance committee needs a well-defined dispute resolution process.

Here are a few more typical data governance issues that businesses deal with.

Controlling internal changes and expectations. Program leaders must set reasonable expectations for development because data governance is frequently a slow process. If not, users and corporate executives may begin to wonder if a program is headed in the correct direction. Significant operational and cultural changes are also a part of many governance projects. If a governance program does not incorporate a strong change management plan, it may result in internal issues and employee resistance.

Regulating large data. The use of big data platforms also presents new governance issues and requirements. Data governance systems used to concentrate on relational database-stored structured data, but they now have to cope with the various forms of data that are commonly found in big data environments, including structured, unstructured, and semi-structured data. These days, a wide range of data platforms are now prevalent, such as cloud object stores, NoSQL databases, and Hadoop and Spark systems. Additionally, data governance is made more difficult by the fact that massive data sets are frequently kept in data lakes in their raw form before being filtered for analytics purposes. This also holds for data lakehouse, a more recent technology that blends aspects of data lakes with conventional data warehouses, which are used to store structured data for analysis.

Supporting analytics for self-service. By giving more users in businesses access to data, the move to self-service BI and analytics has brought forth new data governance issues. In addition to ensuring that data is correct and easily accessible, governance programs must make sure that self-service users—such as business analysts, CEOs, and citizen data scientists—do not abuse data or violate data privacy and security regulations. Streaming data for real-time analytics makes those efforts even more difficult.

Controlling cloud data. Cloud providers oversee some facets of data security and adherence to privacy laws as businesses migrate their current apps and deploy more in the cloud. However, businesses are still in charge of data governance overall, and the same problems that arise with on-premises systems also arise with cloud services. For instance, to prevent privacy compliance difficulties, it may be necessary to keep certain data sets in specific geographic locations and administer them following national laws under the notions of data residency and data sovereignty. This may make it impossible for a business to centralize data and manage it consistently.

Obtaining enough resources and expertise.
Organizations must make sure that the necessary resources are allocated to a governance program, starting at the top level. Involving the appropriate people is also essential. According to Askham, "Appointing the wrong people to key roles can cause the wheels to come off any well-thought-out initiative pretty quickly." In certain situations, it could be essential to bring in outside consultants to assist with an initiative or engage seasoned employees to staff the data governance team.

Implementation of data governance
Organizations should make data governance a strategic priority. The following tasks should be completed as a first step in developing a data governance strategy:

- ✓ Choose a way to gauge the governance program's effectiveness.

- ✓ Determine the data assets and informal governance procedures that are currently in place.
- ✓ Boost end users' data literacy and proficiency.

Before putting a data governance framework into place, it is also necessary to identify the owners or custodians of various data assets throughout an organization and involve them, or chosen surrogates, in the governance program. After that, the CDO, executive sponsor, or specialized data governance manager takes the initiative to design the program's framework. This includes establishing the governance committee, finding data stewards, and staffing the data governance team.

After the framework is established, the actual task of managing data starts. Rules governing the usage of data by authorized staff must be established, as well as data governance policies and standards. To ensure continuous adherence to internal policies and external regulations, as well as to ensure that data is used consistently across applications, a set of controls and audit procedures are also required. The governance team should also keep records of the data's origins, storage location, and security measures against abuse and intrusions.

As was shown in the preceding section, the following components are typically included in data governance initiatives:

- ❖ **Catalog of data.** In order to generate an indexed inventory of available data assets, including information on data lineage, search capabilities, and collaboration tools, data catalogs gather metadata from systems. Data catalogs can also include information regarding data governance policies and automated systems for implementing them.

❖ **Classification and mapping of data.** Documenting data assets and the movement of data within an organization is made easier by mapping the data in systems. Then, various data sets can be categorized according to criteria like whether they include sensitive or personal information. How data governance policies are implemented to specific data sets is influenced by the classifications.

❖ **Glossary for business.** An organization's use of business terms and concepts, such as what makes a customer active, might be defined in a business lexicon. Governance initiatives might benefit from business glossaries, which assist create a consistent language for company data.

Chapter 7

Best practices for overseeing efforts related to data governance

Data governance can become controversial in organizations because it usually places restrictions on how data is handled and used. IT and data management teams often worry that if they lead data governance programs, business users will view them as the "data police." According to industry consultants and experienced data governance managers, programs should be business-driven, with data owners involved and the data governance committee making decisions on standards, policies, and rules. This will encourage business buy-in and prevent resistance to governance policies.

Initiatives must include training and education on data stewardship. Business users and data analysts in particular need to understand privacy laws, data usage guidelines, and their accountability for maintaining data sets' consistency. A data governance program's progress must also be continuously communicated to end users, business managers, and corporate officials. Reports, email newsletters, workshops, and other communication techniques can all be used to address that.

Additional best practices for data governance include implementing privacy and data security regulations as near to the source system as feasible, establishing suitable governance policies at all organizational levels, and routinely reviewing governance policies.

An adaptive data governance model that applies various governance policies and styles to specific business processes is what Gartner analyst Saul Judah has suggested. To successfully regulate data and analytics applications, he has also outlined these seven foundations:

1. A governance procedure and collaborative culture that promotes widespread involvement.

2. Continuous instruction and training, along with systems to assess its efficacy

3. Among the fundamental elements of governance are risk management and data security.

4. transparently making decisions while adhering to moral standards.

5. Data lineage and curation are key components of this trust-based governance approach.

6. Agreement inside the company regarding decision rights and data accountability.

7. Business value and organizational results as the main focus.

Data governance for all times and purposes

✓ Assess, track, and adjust the program on a regular basis to take into account new team positions, modifications to rules and regulations, and new technological platforms.

- ✓ Assure the long-term success of the program for all parties involved by committing to transparency, awareness, communication, and training.

- ✓ List the secondary benefits of the program, such as better communication and teamwork among groups, dissolved data silos, and more pertinent, higher-quality data.

- ✓ Gain customers' trust by granting them authority over their data. Ask for customers' consent before using their data for any other reason, and be open and honest about the company's data privacy policy.

- ✓ Form a virtual compliance team including data practitioners who deal directly with program data sources, such as data architects, software engineers, and business analysts.

✓ Collaborate closely with the security team to guarantee that privacy and data access policies are implemented as close to the source data as feasible.

✓ Use metrics to gauge the success and impact of governance programs, such as the number of participants, the number of data sources, and the enhancement of data quality and reuse.

Important elements of data governance

Several additional aspects of the entire data management process serve as the foundation for data governance programs. These aspects most prominently consist of the following:

❖ **Master the handling of data.** Another field of data management that is closely related to data governance procedures is MDM. To ensure that the data is consistent across various systems within an organization, MDM programs create a master collection of data on clients, goods, and other business entities. Therefore, MDM and data governance go hand in hand. However, because departments and business units have different preferences for how to structure master data, MDM initiatives, like governance programs, can cause disagreement within businesses. Furthermore, MDM's acceptance has been constrained by its complexity. A move toward smaller-scale MDM programs motivated by data governance objectives has been made to make it less burdensome.

❖ **Data management.** A data steward is in charge of some of an organization's data, as was previously said. Data governance policies are also implemented and enforced with the assistance of data stewards. They are frequently subject matter experts in their fields and data-savvy business users. Database administrators, data quality analysts, and other data management specialists work along with data stewards. To determine data needs and problems, they also collaborate with business units.

❖ **Quality of data.** The creation of high-quality data is one of the main motivations for data governance initiatives. For governance activities to be successful, data must be accurate, complete, and consistent across systems. In addition to correcting data mistakes and inconsistencies, data cleansing—also referred to as data scrubbing—correlates and eliminates duplicate instances of the same data elements to standardize the listing of clients or goods across several systems. These capabilities are made possible by data quality tools, which include features like data profiling, parsing, and matching.

Information governance, which is more broadly concerned with the overall use of information within an organization, is related to data governance. Although data governance and information governance are generally seen as distinct fields with related objectives, they can be seen as components of each other at a high level.

Chapter 8

Use cases for data governance.

Managing the data utilized in operational systems, as well as the BI and data science applications that are fed by data warehouses, smaller data marts, and data lakes, depends on effective data governance. In addition to being a crucial part of digital transformation projects, it may help with other business operations including risk management, business process management, and mergers and acquisitions.

Data governance procedures are expected to be used even more frequently as new technologies are developed and the value of data and its applications in businesses continue to grow. Laws like the CCPA and GDPR, as well as well-publicized data breaches, have already made incorporating privacy protections into data governance policies a key component of governance initiatives. Controlling the data generated and utilized by generative AI tools, machine learning algorithms, and other AI technologies is likewise becoming more and more important. By 2027, governance issues would prevent 60% of enterprises from realizing the anticipated economic benefit of AI technologies, according to Gartner.

Tools and suppliers for data governance
Data governance tools are available from several providers. Data management experts like Alation, Ataccama, Collibra, Informatica, OneTrust, Precisely, Quest Software, Rocket Software, Semarchy, Syniti, and Qlik's Talend subsidiary are among them, as are well-known IT suppliers like IBM, Oracle, SAP, and SAS Institute Inc. The governance tools are typically included in larger suites that also include data lineage and metadata management features.

Additionally, to expedite a variety of data governance tasks, including policy enforcement, data classification, and documentation of new data assets, suppliers are now integrating machine learning algorithms, natural language processing capabilities, and AI-driven automation.

Final Thought

No firm can properly manage its data without data governance, which is the foundational function of an enterprise data/information management program. Data governance includes both metadata management and the creation of rules and guidelines for evaluating the quality of data. Data governance is one of the most crucial tasks an organization can carry out to guarantee efficient use of its data and information resources since it involves the creation and application of procedures for controlling organizational usage of data.